50 Vanilla and Chocolate Recipes for Home

By: Kelly Johnson

Table of Contents

Vanilla Recipes

- Classic Vanilla Cake
- Vanilla Pudding
- Vanilla Bean Ice Cream
- Vanilla Cupcakes
- Vanilla Custard
- Vanilla Cheesecake
- Vanilla Shortbread Cookies
- Vanilla Milkshake
- Vanilla Fudge
- Vanilla Pound Cake
- Vanilla Chia Pudding
- French Vanilla Coffee
- Vanilla Yogurt Parfait
- Vanilla Pastry Cream
- Vanilla Soufflé
- Vanilla Rice Pudding
- Vanilla Muffins
- Vanilla Buttercream Frosting
- Vanilla Glazed Donuts
- Vanilla Waffles
- Vanilla Crème Brûlée
- Vanilla Protein Smoothie
- Vanilla Meringue Cookies
- Vanilla Bean Syrup
- Vanilla Panna Cotta

Chocolate Recipes

- Classic Chocolate Cake
- Chocolate Pudding
- Chocolate Ice Cream
- Chocolate Brownies
- Chocolate Chip Cookies

- Chocolate Muffins
- Hot Chocolate
- Chocolate Cheesecake
- Chocolate Truffles
- Chocolate Soufflé
- Chocolate Fudge
- Chocolate Ganache
- Chocolate Lava Cake
- Chocolate Mousse
- Chocolate Cupcakes
- Chocolate Chip Pancakes
- Chocolate Croissants
- Chocolate Fondue
- Chocolate Chip Banana Bread
- Chocolate Tart
- Chocolate Protein Shake
- Chocolate Marshmallow Fudge
- Chocolate Glazed Donuts
- Chocolate Almond Bark
- Chocolate Espresso Brownies

Vanilla Recipes

Classic Vanilla Cake

Ingredients:

- 2 ½ cups all-purpose flour
- 2 ½ tsp baking powder
- ½ tsp salt
- 1 cup unsalted butter, softened
- 2 cups sugar
- 4 eggs
- 1 tbsp vanilla extract
- 1 cup whole milk

Instructions:

1. Preheat oven to 350°F (175°C) and grease two 9-inch cake pans.
2. Whisk together flour, baking powder, and salt.
3. Cream butter and sugar until fluffy. Add eggs one at a time, then vanilla.
4. Alternate adding flour mixture and milk.
5. Divide batter into pans and bake for 30-35 minutes.

Vanilla Pudding

Ingredients:

- 2 cups milk
- ½ cup sugar
- 3 tbsp cornstarch
- 1 tsp vanilla extract

Instructions:

1. In a saucepan, whisk sugar and cornstarch. Slowly add milk and cook over medium heat until thickened.
2. Stir in vanilla and chill before serving.

Vanilla Bean Ice Cream

Ingredients:

- 2 cups heavy cream
- 1 cup whole milk
- ¾ cup sugar
- 1 vanilla bean (or 2 tsp vanilla extract)

Instructions:

1. Split the vanilla bean and scrape out seeds.
2. Whisk together cream, milk, and sugar until sugar dissolves.
3. Add vanilla and churn in an ice cream maker.

Vanilla Cupcakes

Ingredients:

- 1 ½ cups all-purpose flour
- 1 ½ tsp baking powder
- ½ tsp salt
- ½ cup unsalted butter, softened
- ¾ cup sugar
- 2 eggs
- 1 tbsp vanilla extract
- ½ cup whole milk

Instructions:

1. Preheat oven to 350°F (175°C) and line a cupcake tray.
2. Whisk flour, baking powder, and salt.
3. Cream butter and sugar, add eggs one at a time, then vanilla.
4. Alternate adding flour mixture and milk.
5. Fill cupcake liners and bake for 18-20 minutes.

Vanilla Custard

Ingredients:

- 2 cups milk
- ½ cup sugar
- 3 egg yolks
- 2 tbsp cornstarch
- 1 tsp vanilla extract

Instructions:

1. Heat milk and sugar until warm.
2. Whisk egg yolks and cornstarch, then slowly add warm milk.
3. Return to heat and cook until thickened, then stir in vanilla.

Vanilla Cheesecake

Ingredients:

- 2 cups cream cheese
- ¾ cup sugar
- 3 eggs
- 1 tbsp vanilla extract
- 1 cup graham cracker crumbs
- ¼ cup melted butter

Instructions:

1. Preheat oven to 325°F (163°C). Mix crumbs and butter, press into a pan.
2. Beat cream cheese, sugar, eggs, and vanilla. Pour over crust.
3. Bake for 45-50 minutes and chill before serving.

Vanilla Shortbread Cookies

Ingredients:

- 1 cup unsalted butter, softened
- ½ cup sugar
- 2 tsp vanilla extract
- 2 ½ cups all-purpose flour

Instructions:

1. Preheat oven to 350°F (175°C).
2. Cream butter and sugar, then add vanilla and flour.
3. Roll out dough, cut into shapes, and bake for 12-15 minutes.

Vanilla Milkshake

Ingredients:

- 2 cups vanilla ice cream
- 1 cup milk
- 1 tsp vanilla extract

Instructions:

1. Blend all ingredients until smooth.
2. Serve immediately with whipped cream if desired.

Vanilla Fudge

Ingredients:

- 2 cups white chocolate chips
- ½ cup condensed milk
- 1 tsp vanilla extract

Instructions:

1. Melt white chocolate with condensed milk over low heat.
2. Stir in vanilla and pour into a greased pan.
3. Let set before cutting into squares.

Vanilla Pound Cake

Ingredients:

- 2 cups all-purpose flour
- 1 tsp baking powder
- ½ tsp salt
- 1 cup butter, softened
- 1 ½ cups sugar
- 4 eggs
- 2 tsp vanilla extract
- ½ cup milk

Instructions:

1. Preheat oven to 350°F (175°C) and grease a loaf pan.
2. Whisk flour, baking powder, and salt.
3. Cream butter and sugar, add eggs, vanilla, and milk.
4. Pour into pan and bake for 50-60 minutes.

Vanilla Chia Pudding

Ingredients:

- 2 cups milk
- ¼ cup chia seeds
- 2 tbsp honey
- 1 tsp vanilla extract

Instructions:

1. Mix all ingredients in a bowl.
2. Refrigerate overnight until thick.

French Vanilla Coffee

Ingredients:

- 1 cup brewed coffee
- ¼ cup milk or cream
- 1 tbsp vanilla syrup (or ½ tsp vanilla extract + 1 tsp sugar)

Instructions:

1. Brew your favorite coffee.
2. Stir in vanilla syrup (or extract and sugar).
3. Add milk or cream and enjoy.

Vanilla Yogurt Parfait

Ingredients:

- 1 cup vanilla yogurt
- ½ cup granola
- ½ cup fresh berries (strawberries, blueberries, raspberries)
- 1 tsp honey (optional)

Instructions:

1. Layer yogurt, granola, and berries in a glass.
2. Drizzle with honey if desired.
3. Serve immediately.

Vanilla Pastry Cream

Ingredients:

- 2 cups milk
- ½ cup sugar
- 4 egg yolks
- 3 tbsp cornstarch
- 2 tsp vanilla extract
- 2 tbsp butter

Instructions:

1. Heat milk and half the sugar in a saucepan.
2. In a separate bowl, whisk egg yolks, cornstarch, and remaining sugar.
3. Slowly add warm milk to egg mixture, then return to heat and cook until thick.
4. Stir in vanilla and butter, then chill before using.

Vanilla Soufflé

Ingredients:

- 1 cup milk
- ¼ cup sugar
- 3 tbsp flour
- 3 tbsp butter
- 3 eggs, separated
- 1 tsp vanilla extract

Instructions:

1. Preheat oven to 375°F (190°C). Grease ramekins with butter and sugar.
2. Melt butter in a saucepan, add flour, and cook for a minute.
3. Slowly whisk in milk and cook until thickened.
4. Remove from heat, stir in egg yolks and vanilla.
5. Beat egg whites until stiff, then fold into batter.
6. Pour into ramekins and bake for 15-18 minutes until puffed.

Vanilla Rice Pudding

Ingredients:

- 2 cups whole milk
- ½ cup cooked rice
- ¼ cup sugar
- 1 tsp vanilla extract
- ¼ tsp cinnamon (optional)

Instructions:

1. In a saucepan, heat milk, rice, and sugar over low heat.
2. Cook until thick and creamy, about 15-20 minutes.
3. Stir in vanilla and cinnamon, then serve warm or chilled.

Vanilla Muffins

Ingredients:

- 2 cups all-purpose flour
- 1 tbsp baking powder
- ½ tsp salt
- ½ cup unsalted butter, melted
- ¾ cup sugar
- 2 eggs
- 1 tbsp vanilla extract
- 1 cup milk

Instructions:

1. Preheat oven to 350°F (175°C) and line a muffin tin.
2. Mix flour, baking powder, and salt.
3. In a separate bowl, whisk butter, sugar, eggs, vanilla, and milk.
4. Combine wet and dry ingredients, then fill muffin cups.
5. Bake for 18-22 minutes until golden.

Vanilla Buttercream Frosting

Ingredients:

- 1 cup unsalted butter, softened
- 3 cups powdered sugar
- 2 tsp vanilla extract
- 2 tbsp heavy cream

Instructions:

1. Beat butter until creamy.
2. Add powdered sugar, vanilla, and cream, then beat until fluffy.
3. Use to frost cakes, cupcakes, or cookies.

Vanilla Glazed Donuts

Ingredients:

- 2 ½ cups all-purpose flour
- 1 tbsp baking powder
- ½ tsp salt
- ½ cup sugar
- ½ cup milk
- 2 eggs
- ¼ cup unsalted butter, melted
- 1 tbsp vanilla extract

For the Glaze:

- 1 cup powdered sugar
- 2 tbsp milk
- 1 tsp vanilla extract

Instructions:

1. Preheat oven to 350°F (175°C) and grease a donut pan.
2. In a bowl, whisk flour, baking powder, salt, and sugar.
3. In another bowl, mix milk, eggs, butter, and vanilla. Combine wet and dry ingredients.
4. Fill donut molds and bake for 12-15 minutes.
5. Mix glaze ingredients, then dip donuts once cooled.

Vanilla Waffles

Ingredients:

- 2 cups all-purpose flour
- 1 tbsp baking powder
- ½ tsp salt
- 2 tbsp sugar
- 2 eggs
- 1 ¾ cups milk
- ½ cup melted butter
- 1 tbsp vanilla extract

Instructions:

1. Preheat waffle iron and grease with butter or cooking spray.
2. In a bowl, whisk flour, baking powder, salt, and sugar.
3. In another bowl, beat eggs, then add milk, butter, and vanilla.
4. Combine wet and dry ingredients and mix until smooth.
5. Pour batter into waffle iron and cook until golden brown.

Vanilla Crème Brûlée

Ingredients:

- 2 cups heavy cream
- ½ cup sugar
- 4 egg yolks
- 1 vanilla bean (or 2 tsp vanilla extract)
- 2 tbsp sugar (for caramelized top)

Instructions:

1. Preheat oven to 325°F (163°C).
2. Heat cream and vanilla bean in a saucepan until warm.
3. In a bowl, whisk egg yolks and sugar. Gradually add warm cream.
4. Pour into ramekins and place in a water bath.
5. Bake for 35-40 minutes until set. Chill for at least 2 hours.
6. Sprinkle sugar on top and caramelize with a torch.

Vanilla Protein Smoothie

Ingredients:

- 1 cup milk (or almond milk)
- 1 scoop vanilla protein powder
- 1 banana
- 1 tsp vanilla extract
- ½ cup ice

Instructions:

1. Blend all ingredients until smooth.
2. Pour into a glass and enjoy!

Vanilla Meringue Cookies

Ingredients:

- 3 egg whites
- ¾ cup sugar
- 1 tsp vanilla extract
- ¼ tsp cream of tartar

Instructions:

1. Preheat oven to 225°F (110°C) and line a baking sheet.
2. Beat egg whites and cream of tartar until foamy.
3. Gradually add sugar while beating until stiff peaks form.
4. Fold in vanilla, then pipe onto baking sheet.
5. Bake for 1 ½ hours, then cool.

Vanilla Bean Syrup

Ingredients:

- 1 cup water
- 1 cup sugar
- 1 vanilla bean (or 1 tbsp vanilla extract)

Instructions:

1. In a saucepan, heat water and sugar until dissolved.
2. Add vanilla bean seeds and simmer for 5 minutes.
3. Strain and store in a jar.

Vanilla Panna Cotta

Ingredients:

- 2 cups heavy cream
- ½ cup sugar
- 1 vanilla bean (or 2 tsp vanilla extract)
- 1 ½ tsp gelatin
- 2 tbsp cold water

Instructions:

1. In a saucepan, heat cream, sugar, and vanilla.
2. In a small bowl, bloom gelatin with water.
3. Stir gelatin into warm cream until dissolved.
4. Pour into molds and chill for 4 hours.

Chocolate Recipes

Classic Chocolate Cake

Ingredients:

- 2 cups all-purpose flour
- ¾ cup cocoa powder
- 2 tsp baking powder
- 1 ½ tsp baking soda
- ½ tsp salt
- 1 cup sugar
- 1 cup brown sugar
- 2 eggs
- 1 cup buttermilk
- ½ cup vegetable oil
- 2 tsp vanilla extract
- 1 cup hot coffee

Instructions:

1. Preheat oven to 350°F (175°C). Grease two 9-inch cake pans.
2. Mix flour, cocoa powder, baking powder, baking soda, and salt.
3. In another bowl, whisk sugar, eggs, buttermilk, oil, and vanilla.
4. Combine wet and dry ingredients, then stir in hot coffee.
5. Pour into pans and bake for 30-35 minutes.
6. Cool and frost as desired.

Chocolate Pudding

Ingredients:

- 2 cups milk
- ½ cup sugar
- ¼ cup cocoa powder
- 2 tbsp cornstarch
- ¼ tsp salt
- 1 tsp vanilla extract
- ½ cup chopped chocolate

Instructions:

1. Heat milk in a saucepan.
2. Mix sugar, cocoa, cornstarch, and salt in a bowl.
3. Whisk dry mix into warm milk and cook until thick.
4. Remove from heat, add vanilla and chocolate, then stir.
5. Chill before serving.

Chocolate Ice Cream

Ingredients:

- 2 cups heavy cream
- 1 cup whole milk
- ¾ cup sugar
- ½ cup cocoa powder
- 1 tsp vanilla extract
- ½ cup melted chocolate

Instructions:

1. Whisk all ingredients in a saucepan over low heat.
2. Chill mixture, then churn in an ice cream maker.
3. Freeze until firm.

Chocolate Brownies

Ingredients:

- 1 cup melted butter
- 1 ½ cups sugar
- 1 tsp vanilla extract
- 3 eggs
- ¾ cup cocoa powder
- 1 cup flour
- ½ tsp salt
- ½ tsp baking powder

Instructions:

1. Preheat oven to 350°F (175°C). Grease a baking pan.
2. Whisk butter, sugar, vanilla, and eggs.
3. Add cocoa, flour, salt, and baking powder. Mix.
4. Bake for 25-30 minutes.

Chocolate Chip Cookies

Ingredients:

- 2 ¼ cups all-purpose flour
- 1 tsp baking soda
- ½ tsp salt
- 1 cup unsalted butter, softened
- ¾ cup sugar
- ¾ cup brown sugar
- 2 tsp vanilla extract
- 2 eggs
- 2 cups chocolate chips

Instructions:

1. Preheat oven to 350°F (175°C).
2. Cream butter and sugars, then add eggs and vanilla.
3. Stir in flour, baking soda, and salt. Fold in chocolate chips.
4. Bake for 10-12 minutes.

Chocolate Muffins

Ingredients:

- 2 cups flour
- ½ cup cocoa powder
- 1 tbsp baking powder
- ½ tsp salt
- 1 cup sugar
- 2 eggs
- ¾ cup milk
- ½ cup melted butter
- 1 cup chocolate chips

Instructions:

1. Preheat oven to 375°F (190°C).
2. Mix flour, cocoa, baking powder, salt, and sugar.
3. Add eggs, milk, and butter. Stir in chocolate chips.
4. Bake for 18-22 minutes.

Hot Chocolate

Ingredients:

- 2 cups milk
- ½ cup heavy cream
- ¼ cup cocoa powder
- ¼ cup sugar
- ½ tsp vanilla extract
- ½ cup chopped chocolate

Instructions:

1. Heat milk and cream in a saucepan.
2. Whisk in cocoa powder and sugar.
3. Stir in chopped chocolate until melted.
4. Add vanilla and serve warm.

Chocolate Cheesecake

Ingredients:

- 2 cups chocolate cookie crumbs
- ½ cup melted butter
- 2 cups cream cheese, softened
- ¾ cup sugar
- ½ cup cocoa powder
- 3 eggs
- 1 cup sour cream
- 1 tsp vanilla extract

Instructions:

1. Preheat oven to 325°F (163°C).
2. Mix cookie crumbs and butter, press into pan.
3. Beat cream cheese, sugar, and cocoa. Add eggs, sour cream, and vanilla.
4. Pour into crust and bake for 50-55 minutes.

Chocolate Truffles

Ingredients:

- 1 cup heavy cream
- 2 cups dark chocolate, chopped
- 1 tsp vanilla extract
- Cocoa powder, for coating

Instructions:

1. Heat cream, then pour over chopped chocolate.
2. Stir until smooth, add vanilla.
3. Chill until firm, then roll into balls.
4. Coat in cocoa powder.

Chocolate Soufflé

Ingredients:

- 2 tbsp butter (for greasing)
- 2 tbsp sugar (for dusting)
- ½ cup dark chocolate, chopped
- 2 tbsp butter
- 2 tbsp flour
- ½ cup milk
- 2 tbsp sugar
- 2 egg yolks
- 3 egg whites
- ¼ tsp cream of tartar
- 2 tbsp sugar (for meringue)

Instructions:

1. Preheat oven to 375°F (190°C). Grease ramekins and dust with sugar.
2. Melt chocolate and butter together.
3. In a saucepan, whisk flour and milk until thick, then stir in sugar and chocolate mixture.
4. Remove from heat and mix in egg yolks.
5. Whip egg whites with cream of tartar, gradually adding sugar, until stiff peaks form.
6. Gently fold into chocolate mixture, then pour into ramekins.
7. Bake for 12-15 minutes until risen.

Chocolate Fudge

Ingredients:

- 2 cups chocolate chips
- 1 can (14 oz) sweetened condensed milk
- ¼ cup butter
- 1 tsp vanilla extract

Instructions:

1. Melt chocolate, condensed milk, and butter over low heat.
2. Remove from heat, stir in vanilla.
3. Pour into a lined pan and chill for 2 hours.

Chocolate Ganache

Ingredients:

- 1 cup heavy cream
- 1 cup dark chocolate, chopped

Instructions:

1. Heat cream until simmering, then pour over chocolate.
2. Let sit for 2 minutes, then stir until smooth.
3. Use as a glaze, dip, or frosting.

Chocolate Lava Cake

Ingredients:

- ½ cup butter
- 4 oz dark chocolate, chopped
- 2 eggs
- 2 egg yolks
- ¼ cup sugar
- 2 tbsp flour

Instructions:

1. Preheat oven to 425°F (220°C). Grease ramekins.
2. Melt butter and chocolate together.
3. Whisk eggs, yolks, and sugar until pale, then mix in chocolate and flour.
4. Pour into ramekins and bake for 10-12 minutes.
5. Serve warm with ice cream.

Chocolate Mousse

Ingredients:

- 1 cup heavy cream
- ½ cup dark chocolate, melted
- 1 tbsp sugar
- ½ tsp vanilla extract

Instructions:

1. Whip cream, sugar, and vanilla until soft peaks form.
2. Fold in melted chocolate.
3. Chill before serving.

Chocolate Cupcakes

Ingredients:

- 1 cup flour
- ½ cup cocoa powder
- 1 tsp baking powder
- ½ tsp salt
- ½ cup butter
- ¾ cup sugar
- 2 eggs
- ½ cup milk
- 1 tsp vanilla extract

Instructions:

1. Preheat oven to 350°F (175°C).
2. Mix dry ingredients.
3. Beat butter and sugar, then add eggs, milk, and vanilla.
4. Combine with dry ingredients.
5. Bake for 18-20 minutes.

Chocolate Chip Pancakes

Ingredients:

- 1 cup flour
- 1 tbsp sugar
- 1 tsp baking powder
- ½ tsp salt
- 1 cup milk
- 1 egg
- 1 tbsp butter, melted
- ½ cup chocolate chips

Instructions:

1. Mix dry ingredients.
2. Add milk, egg, and butter.
3. Fold in chocolate chips.
4. Cook on a griddle until golden.

Chocolate Croissants

Ingredients:

- 1 sheet puff pastry
- ½ cup chocolate chips
- 1 egg (for egg wash)

Instructions:

1. Preheat oven to 375°F (190°C).
2. Cut puff pastry into triangles.
3. Place chocolate chips in the center and roll into crescents.
4. Brush with egg wash and bake for 15-18 minutes.

Chocolate Fondue

Ingredients:

- 1 cup heavy cream
- 8 oz chocolate, chopped
- 1 tbsp butter
- 1 tsp vanilla extract

Instructions:

1. Heat cream until warm.
2. Stir in chocolate, butter, and vanilla until smooth.
3. Serve with fruits and marshmallows for dipping.

Chocolate Chip Banana Bread

Ingredients:

- 2 ripe bananas, mashed
- ½ cup melted butter
- ¾ cup sugar
- 2 eggs
- 1 tsp vanilla extract
- 1 ½ cups all-purpose flour
- 1 tsp baking soda
- ½ tsp salt
- ½ cup chocolate chips

Instructions:

1. Preheat oven to 350°F (175°C). Grease a loaf pan.
2. Mix bananas, butter, sugar, eggs, and vanilla.
3. Stir in flour, baking soda, and salt. Fold in chocolate chips.
4. Pour into the pan and bake for 50-55 minutes.

Chocolate Tart

Ingredients:

Crust:

- 1 ½ cups crushed chocolate cookies
- ¼ cup melted butter

Filling:

- 1 cup heavy cream
- 8 oz dark chocolate, chopped
- 2 tbsp sugar
- 1 tsp vanilla extract

Instructions:

1. Mix cookie crumbs and melted butter, press into a tart pan, and chill.
2. Heat cream and sugar, pour over chocolate, and stir until smooth.
3. Pour into crust and chill for 2 hours.

Chocolate Protein Shake

Ingredients:

- 1 cup milk (or almond milk)
- 1 scoop chocolate protein powder
- 1 banana
- 1 tbsp cocoa powder
- 1 tbsp peanut butter
- ½ cup ice

Instructions:

1. Blend all ingredients until smooth.
2. Enjoy chilled!

Chocolate Marshmallow Fudge

Ingredients:

- 2 cups chocolate chips
- 1 can (14 oz) sweetened condensed milk
- 1 cup mini marshmallows
- ½ cup chopped nuts (optional)

Instructions:

1. Melt chocolate and condensed milk over low heat.
2. Stir in marshmallows and nuts.
3. Pour into a pan and chill for 2 hours.

Chocolate Glazed Donuts

Ingredients:

- 2 cups flour
- ½ cup sugar
- 2 tsp baking powder
- ½ tsp salt
- ¾ cup milk
- 2 eggs
- ¼ cup melted butter
- 1 tsp vanilla extract

Glaze:

- 1 cup powdered sugar
- ¼ cup cocoa powder
- 3 tbsp milk

Instructions:

1. Preheat oven to 375°F (190°C).
2. Mix dry and wet ingredients separately, then combine.
3. Pour into a donut pan and bake for 12-15 minutes.
4. Whisk glaze ingredients and dip warm donuts in.

Chocolate Almond Bark

Ingredients:

- 2 cups dark chocolate, melted
- 1 cup toasted almonds
- 1 tsp sea salt

Instructions:

1. Mix melted chocolate and almonds.
2. Spread onto a baking sheet and sprinkle with salt.
3. Chill until firm, then break into pieces.

Chocolate Espresso Brownies

Ingredients:

- 1 cup melted butter
- 1 ½ cups sugar
- 1 tsp vanilla extract
- 3 eggs
- ¾ cup cocoa powder
- 1 cup flour
- ½ tsp salt
- ½ tsp baking powder
- 1 tbsp espresso powder

Instructions:

1. Preheat oven to 350°F (175°C). Grease a baking pan.
2. Mix butter, sugar, vanilla, and eggs.
3. Stir in cocoa, flour, salt, baking powder, and espresso powder.
4. Bake for 25-30 minutes.

www.ingramcontent.com/pod-product-compliance
Lightning Source LLC
LaVergne TN
LVHW081507060526
838201LV00056BA/2974